## A CELEBRATION OF THE ISLAND OF KAUA'I

Written by Penny Pence Smith

ISLAND HERITAGE PUBLISHING
*A Division of The Madden Corporation*

*REFLECTIONS OF KAUA'I* ™

ISLAND HERITAGE PUBLISHING
*A Division of The Madden Corporation*
*99-880 Iwaena Street*
*Aiea, Hawaii 96701*
*(808) 487-7299*

Project Director, Dixon J. Smith
Designer and Photography Editor, Paul Turley

First Edition —  Fifth Printing, 1997

Printed in Hong Kong

## TABLE OF CONTENTS

*Satellite view of Hawaiian Island chain, with "Garden Isle" Kaua'i in foreground.*

*KAUA'I HAS A BEAUTY AND AN APPEAL ALL ITS OWN, ONE THAT IS DRAMATICALLY DIFFERENT FROM THAT OF THE OTHER ISLANDS IN THE HAWAIIAN CRESCENT.*

Its warm serenity and spectacular scenery have provided the perfect place for reflection and relaxation since the arrival of the earliest Polynesian settlers.

From the lavender mists over Hanalei's shoreline to the crystal clear stillness of a Kaua'i pond, anyone who has spent time in Kaua'i – whether a few days or a lifetime – can attest to her stunning magnetism.

"Kaua'i is where I come to find peace," says an often- returning visitor from a Northwestern state. "The warmth of the sun and the quiet simplicity of the island gets me back to sanity – gives me a reason to return year after year. I think this may be where my heart really lives."

This book is for those of us who have felt the smiling, sun-warmed beckoning from the radiant spirit and lovely faces of Kaua'i.

*A sterling silver waterfall*
*threads its way down a Kaua'i cliff.*

*" remains intoxicatingly remote "*

This sense of deep and long tradition, wrapped in garden-like beauty and rainbow vistas, has summoned visitors to the island of Kaua'i since its first discovery in the days when volcanoes exploded. Today, Kaua'i remains intoxicatingly remote, calling to visitors from all over the world who seek the opportunity for sunshine and quiet reflection.

*The magical beauty of Hanalei was a memorable feature*
*in the classic movie "South Pacific."*

*" Its sparkling beaches...*
*remain some of the most beautiful and uncrowded "*

*Quiet waters reflect a deep spirit.*

*Horseback riders capture the last rays of sunset.*

Its sparkling beaches – warmed by the noon-day sun and surrounded by jungle-like terrain – remain some of the most beautiful and un-crowded among Hawai'i's more populated islands. Waterfalls and secluded pools are neighbors to its peaks and valleys and sparkle through thick tropical forests. Yet underlying the peaceful demeanor of Kaua'i is the vivid and pulsating character of its ancestry – colorful, exciting and passionate.

*Kaua'i has become the perfect place for families to enjoy a sunny respite from everyday life.*

*Ancient salt ponds at Hanapēpē are tended today by nearby residents.*

*" 'Menehunes' were at work building "*

The essence of Kauaʻi, as that of all the Hawaiian islands, is evidenced on three levels: through its ancient myths, through its history, and through the eyes of the people who live and love their home known as "The Garden Island."

It was Kauaʻi that first enchanted the fiery volcano goddess Pele, and enticed her to seek her initial Hawaiʻi home near Hāʻena. There, she danced a passionate love dance on the beach at Kēʻē.

While Pele and the other gods were at work creating the soul and spirit of Kauaʻi, a nation of little people called "Menehune" were at work building its roads, walls, ponds and viaducts. The actual existence of this population of little people is still in contention. Some anthropologists attribute them to tall tales and imagination, and others emphatically point to evidence that they inhabited the islands.

*Intricate rock formations are part of the spectacle of Waimea Canyon.*

Some historians say that the word "*Menehune*" came from the Tahitian word referring to Marquesan Islanders who arrived in Hawai'i prior to the Tahitian migration. Others point to the use of the Tahitian word "*manahune*" referring to commoners – reputedly a logical connection since commoners in Tahiti were not fed as well as the royalty, and were consequently shorter in physical stature.

*" Marquesan Islanders who arrived in Hawai'i "*

*The Polynesians journeyed to Kaua'i on sailing canoes. Today, paddling is still an important part of the culture.*

*Waves and weather have carved the majestic cliffs of Nā Pali.*

*Salt pans in the lava at 'Anini Beach.*

Whatever their origins, the Menehune worked only at night, and hid in the forest during the day. Their structures were built from stones, carved to fit together so precisely that experts today have a difficult time understanding how such expertise and technology could have been developed in early Polynesia.

*Sheer cliffs, sculpted by weather and time, create the dramatic Nā Pali coastline.*

*Menehune were said to have built this ditch.*

## " Their migration to other islands "

Additionally, Menehune were said to have worked in double rows, passing the carved stones from person to person until a structure was complete. Legend says they never returned to the site of a structure once work stopped. Consequently, if a project was not complete when the sun rose, it would never be. Although many of the structures attributed to the Menehune's work are in ruins today, enough of their fine stonemasonry still stands throughout Kaua'i. Their migration to other islands is evidenced both through legend and ancient stonemasonry located in other areas.

*Kaua'i's history can be found in stone artifacts.*

*Canoe racing
is one of the island's most popular sports activities.*

Whoever the Menehune really were, samples of their Kaua'i work still stand in Waimea Canyon, near Lihu'e in Alekoko Fishpond, and in a dam on the Hulē'ia River.

The existence of Fire goddess Pele has never been questioned because her volcanic influence was central to the development of Kaua'i, as it was to the other islands in the Hawaiian Chain. The flamboyant goddess was said to have been born in the form of a flame, the passionate manifestation of love between earth mother *Haumea* and sky father *Wakea*.

Pele's heat is forever present on the island of Kaua'i, because, as with all the Hawaiian islands, Kaua'i's highest point is the top of a volcanic crater. And, the foundation for all life on the island is the solidified lava from the crater.

*An exciting fire dance reflects the ancient messages of Kaua'i.*

*" born in the form of a flame "*

The 'Ohi'a tree keeps vigil over the Waimea Canyon at the Pu'uhinahina Lookout.

*" the wettest place on earth "*

*Fog blankets Waimea Canyon.*

Kawaikini, Kaua'i's highest point, rises 5,243 feet above sea level as part of Mount Wai'ale'ale. This imposing volcano reaching high into the mists and clouds, forever watches over Kaua'i and from the earliest days of the Polynesians established it as a place of solitary, magical power. Wai'ale'ale is considered the wettest place on earth today, its summit nearly always wrapped in a cloak of sterling clouds.

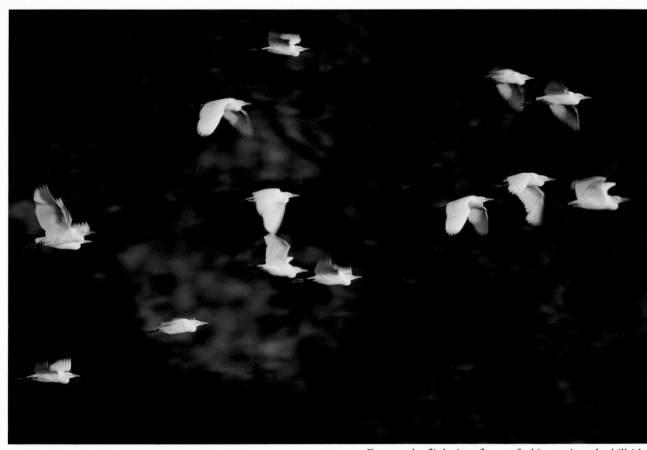

*Egrets take flight in a flurry of white against the hillside.*

Atop the summit, the winds and rain have coupled to create a hidden refuge for rare plants and birds. In fact, a pond shimmering at the peak gave its name to the mountain – *Wai'ale'ale* – A Rippling on the Water.

*A lush Koa forest at sunset.*

It is a rippling that meanders down the hillsides seeking the company of warmer and more genial company. In places it tumbles gently through fern-covered creek beds. In other places it gains momentum, rushing over cliffs and through rocky crevices. Finally, it flows happily through flat farmlands to the sea.

The island of Kaua'i occupies 677 square miles and is at the northwest end of the Hawaiian chain. This leeward location, protected by the stormy Kaua'i Channel, for many decades allowed the people of Kaua'i to remain an independent entity, secluded from the activity of the other islands. Even today it is the least populated of the four major islands, and the one most often sought for its tranquil quiet.

*" rushing over cliffs and through rocky crevices "*

*Hanakāpī'a Falls.*

19

*" its chieftains were
considered some of
the most sacred "*

*The recreated Polynesian sailing vessel "Hōkūleʻa" captures the lore and technology of ancient seafarers.*

Kauaʻi is believed to be the oldest and the earliest populated of the Hawaiian Islands – from the arrival of Pele on her shores, to that of immigrants from the Marquesas, the earliest wave of which is believed to have landed on Kauaʻi. These intrepid seafarers probably landed about 500 A.D. By 750 A.D., all of the islands were thought to have been inhabited by these immigrants. A second wave of migration began again in about 1000 A.D.

Because Kauaʻi was settled so early, its chieftains were considered some of the most sacred, eagerly sought after as potential spouses for *Aliʻi* – royalty – of other islands. The royalty bloodline of Kauaʻi was considered the purest and most desirable.

*Dancers entertain visitors at Kauaʻi resorts with renditions of ancient hulas.*

*" the last outpost for families of Hawaiian lineage "*

*An historic village on the banks of the Wailua River.*

The first arrival of Polynesians took place at the mouth of the Wailua River, subsequently decreed "Sacred" by the chiefs. Small villages of thatched huts were built along the river, accompanied by a series of temples, or *heiaus*. A major heiau was also constructed on top of Mount Wai'ale'ale to honor and worship the all powerful god, *Kāne*.

The island provided all the resources these hearty travellers could desire: flat lands on which to construct homes and villages; waterways where their canoes could be maneuvered easily and safely; forests with wildlife; and the ever abundant sea for fishing. Here on Kaua'i the essence of Hawai'i's ancient lifestyle was established and thrived for a longer time than on any other major island. And it was no surprise that nearby Ni'ihau became the last outpost for families of Hawaiian lineage.

*Traditional seed leis.*

The peaceful, pastoral existence of the ancient Hawaiians on Kaua'i was to be forever interrupted by the arrival of explorer Captain James Cook. His presence on each Hawaiian island signaled a new era, and Kaua'i was no different. The changes came less quickly on Kaua'i, however, because of its inaccessibility.

The ships of Captain James Cook appeared off the coast of Kaua'i in January of 1778. Captain Cook, whose light colored skin and date of arrival coinciding with the celebration of the god *Lono*, was immediately accorded the persona of a god. Yet he spent only a few days exploring the island as Kaua'i's turbulent channel and mischievous weather sent him and his two ships, the Resolution and the Discovery, out to sea for saftey. After several thwarted attempts to return to the island, Cook set sail for other destinations.

*The historic Wailua River as it etches a path to the sea.*

*A perfect Kaua'i day.*

25

*A remnant of the once plentiful Sandlewood forests.*

*" He gifted the Waimea Chief with the first sheep and horned cattle "*

Seven years later, Captain George Vancouver, a former ship's mate with Cook, arrived to explore Kaua'i. He gifted the Waimea Chief with the first sheep and horned cattle, and was also said to have provided seeds for various plants, vines, nuts and citrus samples. Vancouver struck a warm relationship with the people of Kaua'i, and during his stay noted great opportunity in the exportation of sandalwood.

This observation was to be prophetic. Over time, sandalwood traders eventually stripped the forests not only from Kaua'i but from other islands. The ecological results remain a source of concern, even today, to island biologists, conservationists and historians.

27

Vancouver's introduction of horses and cattle was to become another of his prophetic influences on the islands. Ranching ultimately became a way of life on Kaua'i as well as on other islands.

Vancouver returned several times to Kaua'i before returning to his native England in 1794. He left a strong mark on the island people, so much so that Kaua'i's King Kaumauli'i wished to be called "King George." Through Vancouver, close ties were created between Great Britain and Hawai'i.

*The Waioli Mission House in Hanalei is a relic of Kaua'i's historic missionary days.*

*" He left a strong mark on the island people "*

*Tall masts off Kaua'i's coast are an echo of another era.*

*" allowed Russian traders
to construct a fort at the mouth
of the Waimea River "*

*Sunset paints highlights on the Kalalau Valley.*

Kaumuali'i, Kaua'i's last great king, struggled diligently to maintain peace and distance from the rapidly changing political scenario of Hawai'i by maintaining distance from the warring Kamehameha. Kaumuali'i later signed a treaty with Kamehameha, but then broke it in 1816 when he allowed Russian traders to construct a fort at the mouth of the Waimea River. The venture itself was short-lived, but ultimately caused the islanders and their chief a great deal of conflict with the island-wide Ali'i, a story explored more fully in our chapter on Waimea.

*A starburst of palm trees against the Kaua'i sky.*

*" plantations sprung up throughout the island "*

Sugar cane fields gradually replaced the diminishing sandalwood groves, as entrepreneurs saw the promise in the wild cane which the natives grew, primarily as wind breaks. Ladd and Company, the island's first major sugar operation, was established at Koloa in 1837, and other plantations sprung up throughout the island. Names such as George Wilcox, Paul Isenberg, Henry Pierce, Wyllie and McBryde became synonymous with sugar, and are a part of Kaua'i's history woven throughout the following chapters.

*A sugar worker in the fields of McBryde Sugar.*

*Night work in the cane fields.*

*A herd of cattle share the landscape with another tradition on Kauaʻi – sugar cane.*

*Today's ranching techniques don't look much different than those from the early part of the century on Kaua'i.*

Ranching also became common on Kauaʻi, and was extended to the nearby island of Niʻihau by the Sinclair family. Where their descendants, the Robinsons, still maintain the ranchlands on Kauaʻi and Niʻihau, and a generation of "*paniolos*," or Hawaiian cowboys, has grown up, rivaling the salty cowboy life anywhere in the western and southwestern U.S. Mainland.

In 1830, Hawaiʻi's king brought Mexican vaqueros from California to teach islanders how to ride and be ranch hands. From these unlikely beginnings, Hawaiʻi's paniolos have become renowned sport figures at national rodeos, as well as part and parcel of the rustic life that still graces much of Hawaiʻi.

Kauaʻi's paniolos are evident throughout the island, and strut their best stuff each August at the Hanalei Stampede Rodeo.

*" rivaling the salty cowboy life anywhere "*

*Kauaʻi's colorful paniolos
ride the range in their unique, traditional garb.*

Sugar and ranching play an important role in Kaua'i's economy today, as do crops such as papaya and guava. Taro chips are even produced near Waimea. But as with all of the islands, tourism has become of key importance to Kaua'i's growth.

*" tourism has become of key importance "*

*Kaua'i visitors have found her sunny warmth an appealing reason to spend time on Kaua'i.*

*Taro remains an important Kaua'i crop – but not so plentiful as the yearly crop of tourists.*

*Resorts line the shore of Kaua'i like a sparkling necklace.*

37

*Exotic relaxation is the order of the day for guests at Kaua'i Hilton Beach Villas.*

*Princeville Hotel has brought a sense of elegance to Hanalei.*

Because of the proximity of the airport, Lihu'e has become the business center of Kaua'i. On the sunny shores of Po'ipū Beach, pleasant condominiums rest side by side with elegant hotels. Such is also the case at Princeville and Hanalei Bay, which today remains the serene and unspoiled paradise that it seemed when it was called Bali Hai in the movie, *South Pacific*, so many years ago.

*" called Bali Hai in the movie, South Pacific "*

*Leis made of orchids and plumerias are special to visitors – and part of Kauaʻi's everyday culture.*

*" Golf has become a major pastime on Kaua'i – with world class courses dotting the hillsides at Princeville, Kiahuna, Nāwiliwili Bay, Kalāheo and Wailua."*

*The perfect putt executed at Princeville.*

*Kaua'i's golf courses offer a wonderland-type landscape.*

*A vibrant red is one of Kaua'i's many hues.*

*" a reputation for its floral industry "*

*Orchid fields against a Kapaʻa sky.*

Kauaʻi has developed its own community of artists and craftspeople, many of whom show their wares in and around Kapaʻa, and in other locales as well. Jewelery designers, ceramicists, quilters, fashion designers and painters have chosen Kauaʻi as a home base because of the serene, creative atmosphere in which to work.

Kauaʻi has also gained a reputation for its floral industry. Tropical flowers, especially red and pink gingers and heliconias, are grown on small farms around the island, then shipped to Honolulu and other world-wide flower markets. Kauaʻi's farmers credit the balmy weather and the abundance of water for their ability to produce several unique tropical ginger species.

Although a bouquet of lively, contemporary resorts circles much of Kauaʻi, and Lihuʻe and Kapaʻa grow as commerce centers, Kauaʻi remains essentially a quiet and often rural society.

43

" they also study the
ancient songs, dances and crafts "

A young Hawaiian girl
with plumeria headdress and lei.

Many of the island's young people who attend the modern schools sprinkled throughout the island participate as much in a contemporary lifestyle as any young American today. But they also study the ancient songs, dances and crafts of their ancestors. The hula *Hālaus* – or dance schools – of Kaua'i prepare diligently each year to compete in the annual Merrie Monarch Festival, testing their skills and commitment at recreating the ancient hula forms.

*Children learn the ancient art of hula at an early age.*

*The beauty of Hawaiian children never changes.*

Windsurfing has become one of Hawai'i's most popular sports.

*Dressed for a traditional May Day school program.*

Almost as often as youngsters windsurf, or compete in soccer matches and football games, they participate in Hawaiian canoe races. Ardently stroking through the challenging waters from Kealai Bay to Kalapakī Bay each March, the annual "Ironman" Prince Kuhio Race partners teenage paddlers with oldsters.

In the summertime, young Japanese-Hawaiians participate in the *O-Bon* festivals where colorful traditional garb is donned, and rhythmic dances are performed in honor of the ancestral dead.

*Preparing the canoe for a race.*

*" Kauaians know they are special "*

Kaua'i also remains the center of pure Hawaiiana through its cousin Ni'ihau, and through the faces of the children growing up on colorful farms in communities founded on a simple, rural character and attitude. Even without the influx of visitors each year, Kauaians know they are special. The island's spirit and soul are intractably linked with the ancient values and vivid character that typified its ancestors nearly 1500 years ago.

That spirit, along with the breathtaking beauty of the island, attracted Pele to Kaua'i and still has a seductive appeal to visitors from many cultures.

*Kaua'i's pageantry is as colorful as it is traditional.*

*Beautiful Wailua Beach beckoned to ancient surf lovers as well as to today's water enthusiasts.*

*Remnants of yesterday's lifestyle in Koloa Town.*

*REFLECTIONS
FROM THE TOP OF
THE SACRED MOUNTAIN –
AN ISLAND IS BORN*

Standing guard over the island of
Kauaʻi is the imposing Mount
Waiʻaleʻale, the rugged, towering
remainder of the volcano that formed
the island many centuries ago. Then, as
now, the mist-enshrouded summit and
its sentry-like dominance of the island
made it a sacred and revered place.

*" only those with a stout heart – and a commitment – ever explore "*

Wai'ale'ale began forming the island more than five million years ago from a crater that today has an outer rim nearly 10-12 miles in diameter. Centuries of overgrowth have covered the ash and debris of the caldera and made it virtually impossible to find the center-most point of the volcano.

Indeed, the summit of Wai'ale'ale is a place where only those with a stout heart – and a commitment – ever explore. The northern summit of Wai'ale'ale perches 5,150 feet in the sky and collects approximately 460 inches of rain every year, more than anywhere else on earth. This moisture creates the many silver streams of water that cascade down the mountainsides, feed into the many rivers and streams and are responsible for the verdantly beautiful garden environment of the island.

*A thick carpet of foliage covers the top of the mountain.*

*A rare 'apapane bird rests on a bed of colorful streptosolon.*

*" developed
'snowshoe-like' hooves "*

Locked in a demonic dance with the rain, the wind aims fiercely at the rugged northern cliffs of the mountain, often driving the rain back up the rocks to fall again some distance away. Black mosses and lichens cover the floor of the summit, making foot travel uncertain. Miniaturized rare plants are tucked into crevices and valleys. These are plants such as tiny violets, rare asters and geraniums, even a lily with foliage resembling swords, unique to Kaua'i. The ferocity of the elements have apparently dwarfed all of the vegetation in this area – trees, bushes as well as flowering species.

Local stories tell of cattle that strayed upwards onto the heights of the mountain and when discovered many months later, had developed "snow-shoe-like" hooves to handle the wet, mossy terrain.

The banana poka flower catches the afternoon light.

Cattle from nearby ranches
graze on the slopes of Wai'ale'ale.

The northern precipice is banked with rare 'ape'ape plants and drops 2,500 feet into the valley below. On that precipice, between two knolls, is an imposing ancient *heiau*, an altar, known as Ka'awakō, where it is believed that only the chosen few were allowed to worship. The altar stood two feet high, five feet wide and seven feet long with a tall, obelisk like object at the rear. A short distance away, a shallow pond shimmers in the wind and gives the mountain its name – *A Rippling on the Water*.

Water flows from the sacred pond into the Waini ha Valley on Kaua'i's north side, and through the engineering efforts of the early Hawaiians, a ditch from the plateau's western sector connects the Wailua River with the mystical waters of Wai'ale'ale.

On the western side of the mountain, at Wai'ale'ale's highest point, Kawaikini, is the Alaka'i Swamp, Kaua'i's great watershed source which feeds its rivers and streams. Approximately thirty miles square, the Alaka'i Swamp extends nearly to the sea. Early Hawaiians irrigated their crops with the waters from the swamp and constantly gave thanks to their god Kāne for providing them with this seemingly endless supply of "living waters."

*" A Rippling on the Water "*

All of the contours of Mt. Wai'ale'ale are dramatic.

*Wai'ale'ale's rainfall is a major reason for Kaua'i's beautiful garden environment.*

*SUNSHINE*
*REFLECTED ON*
*QUIET WATERS –*
*KAUA'I 'S WESTERN SHORES*

Flowing from the waters of the Alaka'i Swamp
are those streams that join to create the Waimea
River, the longest river in Hawai'i which flows
through the spectacular Waimea Canyon.

It is the very nature of Kaua'i to have etched
out this moment of natural drama within such
an exotic garden-like environment.

*The unusual Iliau plant stands as a sentry over the*
*Waimea Canyon.*

59

*The "fiddle fern" is endemic to the islands.*

Waimea Canyon, twelve miles long and three thousand feet deep, has often been called the Grand Canyon of the Pacific. Like its southwestern U.S. name-sake, the rush to view its many panoramas has made it Kaua'i's most frequently requested sightseeing spot. Today, helicopters bearing visitors from all over the world dip and peek into the many dramatic crevices, soar against the rugged Nā Pali Cliffs nearby and afford passengers a spectacular view as well as an exhilarating experience.

*Waimea Canyon is a wonderland for naturalists.*

*" Grand Canyon of the Pacific "*

*The Canyon is Kaua'i's most sought-after attraction.*

*Visitors view the canyon from a lookout post.*

*" created by the effect
of water and wind on the slopes of Mount Wai'ale'ale "*

Waimea Canyon, however, is still in transformation. Its dimensions were created by the effect of water and wind on the slopes of Mount Wai'ale'ale, breaking down the lava formations until deep gorges and lofty peaks were etched. Erosion continues to change the face of Waimea Canyon – subtly in some areas, more obviously in others. The head of the canyon, for example, is reportedly eroding toward the head of the Kalalau Valley along the Nā Pali Coast and they are anticipated to meet in the not too distant future.

*Every aspect of Waimea Canyon is magnificent.*

Along the canyon ridges one can see Kaua'i's *"paniolos"* or cowboys, riding herd on cattle. With their colorful tropical bandanas and hats, these latterday cowpokes are part and parcel of Kaua'i – whether keeping watch over their herds along the ridges of Waimea Canyon, competing in the annual Hanalei Stampede, or keeping colorful vigil around Koloa Town.

*The entire family gets into the act on rodeo day.*

*" Kaua'i's 'paniolos' or cowboys "*

*A paniolo way of life is evident throughout Kaua'i.*

*" that reflect the lifestyle of the early  paniolos "*

In Kōke'e State Park, a major gateway to Waimea Canyon, a rustic lodge boasts cabins that reflect the lifestyle of the early paniolos – complete with fireplaces to warm a cool evening at the higher altitudes and lantern light for reading. The Natural History Museum at Kōke'e is a popular stopping place for visitors to catch an overall glimpse of the area's history.

*The historic Kōke'e Lodge is a favorite stopping spot.*

*Air National Guard facility at Kōke'e.*

*A lone rider at Kōke'e.*

*" creating their bright traditional ceremonial cloaks "*

*Mountain goats are familiar residents on the slopes of the canyon.*

Kōke‘e is also a home to some of the state's most beautiful bird species – including the exotic ‘I‘iwi. Ancient Ali‘i and warriors collected the feathers from the colorful ‘I‘iwi and used them for creating their bright traditional ceremonial cloaks. These cloaks were of great importance to their owners for they marked the stature of an individual. The longer the cloak, the greater the importance of the wearer.

The delicate Anianiau, which perches against the dramatic Kōke‘e land-scape in yellow and green hues, is found only on the island of Kaua‘i.

*Exotic birds are part of Kaua‘i's charm.*

*Plant life in many canyon areas have adapted to the desert-like enviornment.*

*Sunset infuses highlights around Kaʻula Island off Niʻihau.*

*There is a desert-like beauty around Poiʻpū.*

Waimea Canyon opens into the pristine beaches at the edge of the Nā Pali Coast, from Sacred Springs to the town of Waimea, where Captain James Cook first set foot on the island.

At the farthest end of the main roadway is Polihale State Park, a quiet, lovely beach nestled at the base of the cliffs. From this beach one can look across the channel to Niʻihau, an island dedicated to pure Hawaiian families.

*The serenity of a Kauaʻi sunset.*

*" one can look across the channel to Niʻihau "*

*" a small,*
*traditional sugar plantation town "*

Fields of cane carve a unique pattern of green.

The business of agriculture has a beauty all its own.

Two ancient heiau reside nearby Polihale, along with a sacred pond. Kekaha is a small, traditional sugar plantation town with a mill as its center point. Kekaha is a key entrance to Waimea Canyon, and is the only available commercial center along this coast. In ancient times, however, there were said to have been several small villages spread out along the coastline.

*Plantations today still retain their classic charm.*

*Cane trucks stir up a colorful scene against the sea.* 73

*" a sophisticated ditch system "*

*Menehune are said to have built this fishpond.*

Just outside of Waimea is a valley now covered with weeds and forest, which once housed taro farms irrigated by means of a sophisticated ditch system, said to have been built by Menehune.

Waimea itself is one of Hawai'i's oldest towns and was the site where Captain James Cook initially landed in 1778. It was also the site where the first missionaries on Kaua'i landed in May of 1820.

*An afternoon's work in the taro patches.*

*Captain Cook's landing site gives a clue as to why he was enthralled by Kaua'i.*

*The Koloa Missionary Church in Koloa Town.*

Embarking originally from Boston Harbor, the ship *Thaddeus* arrived, following an initial stop in Honolulu which was established as the seat of the Christian missionary activity in the Sandwich Islands. When the *Thaddeus* reached Kaua'i, three missionaries were aboard – one of them young George Kaumuali'i, son of Kaua'i's King Kaumuali'i.

From the deck of the *Thaddeus*, the newcomers were awestruck with the beauty of the coastline. On shore, a warm and affectionate reunion took place between King Kaumuali'i and his son. "…his father rose, clasped him in his arms, and pressed his nose to his son's after the manner of the country…I know not when I have wept more freely," wrote Missionary Samuel Ruggles of the moment.

*" a warm and affectionate reunion took place "*

*Religion still plays an important role in the islands.*

*" a mission station*
*was in order for Kaua'i "*

It is no surprise that the King opened his heart
and his homeland to these strangers and it was
decided almost immediately in Honolulu that a
mission station was in order for Kaua'i. In July
of 1820, two missionary families, Samuel and
Nancy Ruggles, and Samuel and Mercy Whitney
arrived to establish their homes. In October,
Mercy Whitney gave birth to the first white
child born in the Hawaiian islands.

*Much of Koloa Town has been preserved.*

*The pattern for a Hawaiian quilt.*

*A typical shopping list for missionaries to Hawai'i.*

By the year's end, the missionary families were already making sugar and molasses from the cane growing so profusely around them. In Waimea, the local population also continued to cultivate taro and yams, and had unlimited access to coconuts and bananas as well as sugar cane.

Kaua'i's oldest missionary home, the Gulick-Rowell House, still occupies a place of prominence in Waimea, open for visitors to view a glimpse of the simple lifestyle that existed during this important time of transition in the island's history.

Hawaiian quilt makers have created their own unique artform.    81

Waimea was also the site of Kaua'i's railroad, established in 1881, when a locomotive and cars were imported from Germany to carry sugar cane between Waimea and Kekaha and other plantations. A young Liliuokalani, who was to be Hawai'i's last reigning monarch, drove the first spike in the track in September of 1880.

Just as the Hawaiians and the earliest missionaries gained access to Waimea Canyon through Waimea, today's explorers and visitor use this historic point as the gateway to the canyon and Kōke'e State Park.

A few minutes from Waimea are the remains of Fort Elizabeth, a "Fort" built in 1815 by a Russian named George Scheffer and a group of his countrymen. The fort was constructed by Scheffer's Russian-American Company through an alliance with King Kaumuali'i. But confidence in the alliance and its long term intentions faltered quickly. According to most accounts the fort was an effort by the Russian government to gain a stronghold in the Pacific, but no support from Moscow was accorded to Waimea's Russian group. Within two short years, the Kings of Hawai'i had overruled Kaumuali'i, deposed Scheffer and his men and taken possession of the "Fort." It was dismantled in 1864.

*The picturesque tunnel of trees near Koloa.*

*" Hawaiians and the earliest missionaries "*

*Poi'pū's Ka'ahumanu Society celebrates Kuhio Day.*

*" a picturesque portrait of a quieter Hawai'i "*

The Waimea River and its surrounding streams have helped this southern area of Kaua'i become a source of food through its colorful rural farms. The quaint town of Hanapēpē, nestled next to the Hanapēpē River, is a picturesque portrait of a quieter Hawai'i than most know in the more visible, populated areas. Taro patches and other agricultural crops sweep to the red cliffs that delineate the boundaries of the lovely Hanapēpē Canyon. It is also a place where much of the lifestyle has not changed since the earliest days.

For example, the Salt Pond Beach Park near Hanapēpē, is a place where local families still come to collect rock salt through methods used by their ancestors. Brownish in color, the salt is not sold on the open market, but used by those friends and neighbors of the saltmakers.

At the turn of the century, Hanapēpē was a draw to Asian immigrants who planted rice paddies and established themselves as traders with other island merchants and farmers.

*A heron regards life in his favorite taro patch.*

*Local Japanese women celebrate May Day.*

*Fishing is still part of life here.*

*" its reputation for
pastoral productivity and beauty "*

*Petroglyphs tell of life in ancient times.*

In addition to its reputation for pastoral productivity and beauty, Hanapēpē carries an important slice of Hawaiian history. In 1824, King Kaumuali'i's son Humehume waged a last bloody battle to retain independence for Kaua'i against King Kamehameha II. In a spot about opposite Hanapēpē Canyon Lookout, Humehume led his rebels against the Kamehameha loyalists and when the battle ended, the bodies of more than 100 Kauaian warriors were reportedly strewn through the valley. Humehume was captured and imprisoned.

*Two friends spend good times together.*

*Hula hands tell stories of old Hawai'i.*

It was not a good year for the elder Kaumuali'i, either, who two years prior had been forced into marriage with Ka'ahumanu, widow of Kamehameha the Great and one of the most powerful Ali'i in the Islands. Because Kauaian royalty was considered to have the purest of Hawaiian blood, and Kaumuali'i had an excellent reputation among his people, he was deemed to be an appropriate mate for the important Ka'ahumanu.

In 1824, however, he died essentially "in captivity," leaving great sorrow among his people. The Reverend Hiram Bingham wrote of him, "he was sedate, dignified, courteous in his manners, honorable in his dealings, respected by foreigners, highly esteemed by the missionaries, and beloved by his people."

*" leaving great sorrow among his people "*

*Kalāheo Catholic Church against the sunset.*

*Hanapēpē.*

Today, the farmlands around Hanapēpē, inland at Kalāheo and at Lāwaʻi Kai are part of the frescos that have given Kauaʻi the name "Garden Isle." Colorfully vivid botanical gardens welcome thousands of visitors each year.

On the estate of the former Kauaʻi Pineapple Company is the ʻOlu Pua Botanical Garden, and on the former Walter Sinclair McBryde estate is Kukui o Lono Park which boasts spectacular views of the ocean as well as a nine-hole golf course. In the lush and emerald Lāwaʻi Valley is the Pacific Tropical Botanical Gardens, 186 acres of plant species collected from throughout the world. On the property adjacent is the Allerton Gardens at Lāwaʻi Kai, beautiful gardens surrounding the summer cottage of Queen Emma, wife of Kamehameha IV.

*A botanist examines rare plants.*

Not far away is one of the island's most popular and unique natural wonders – the spouting horn, a lava tube which catches the force of the incoming waves and shoots the water high into the air. At one time a much larger horn blew its briny contents across the existing road and into the nearby plantation fields. The plantation management dynamited the rock tunnel because the salt water killed the valuable sugar cane.

This golden coast is the favorite home for sun seekers on Kaua'i. Poi'pū Beach, once a whaler's destination, is now a cozy crescent of hotels and condominiums, adding a spritely, contemporary exclamation mark to this historic and dramatic coastline. At Poi'pū, international visitors  enjoy the soft warmth of the Kaua'i sun as it spills hospitably onto the bleached sands and lights the craggy reefs that flirt with the shoreline.

*Elegant dining awaits guests*
*at Stouffer Waiohai Beach Resort.*

*Poi'pū is an enchanting treat for beach-lovers.*

*Watersports abound at Poiʻpū.*

*Captivating Poiʻpū.*

95

*A sea creature watches curiously as divers explore.*

*The waters of Poiʻpū are filled with underwater fantasies.*

*" vividly colorful undersea delights "*

One of Hawai'i's most opulent scuba diving caverns is just off the shore at Poi'pū. Known as the Sheraton Caverns because of its proximity to the Sheraton–Kaua'i beach, this underwater wonderland offers three "rooms" 35-60 feet deep, filled with vividly colorful undersea delights. Among them are green sea turtles that have a penchant for swimming with the scuba divers and bringing startled joy to newcomers in this underwater world. An adjoining chamber is known as the "lobster nursery" because of the many types of spiny residents living there.

*The venerable sea turtle, a protected species, often joins visitors for a swim.*

*" in historic Koloa Town"*

Part of the history of Kaua'i is deeply entrenched in sugar cane operations which began only a few miles north of Poi'pū in historic Koloa Town. Today it is a charmingly restored collection of retail boutiques, shops and food services. But Koloa Town was originally the center of all sugar operations for Kaua'i and, in fact, was the site of Kaua'i's first successful sugar mill.

William Ladd, William Hooper, and Peter Allen Brinsmade, three New Englanders with an eye to the commercial possibilities of sugar on Kaua'i, leased from Kamehameha III 980 acres of land at Koloa. The proximity of the nearby Ma'ulili Waterfall allowed the team to dam the waters to create power. The crop yield of the newly formed Ladd and Company's first harvest was lucrative and by 1841, a larger facility was required and constructed nearby.

*Interesting shops and stores are evident throughout Kaua'i.*

*Old Koloa Town has always enjoyed the air of celebration.*

*Equestrian history is alive and well in Koloa.*

*A sugar mill in operation.*

*" printing up its own currency "*

*On the McBryde Sugar Plantation.*

The Ladd and Company sugar operations were the centrifugal force for the town of Koloa for nearly a century, at one point printing up its own currency paid to sugar workers to be spent in the company stores. In 1913 a new mill was built in Ka'a, about a mile away from the previous mill. Over the years various commercial entities have acquired and merged to form the cane operations now leased by a Mainland firm.

Smaller, independent sugar mills were also established around the area as well. One of them kept a small dungeon for the retention of unruly workers.

Only a few stone walls remain from the 1841 Ladd and Company boiling houses, but Koloa Town reflects its ambitious heritage – a tradition evident along the entire Western shoreline inland to Koloa.

Resting quietly a few miles off Kaua'i's western shores is the island of Ni'ihau – the last stronghold of the Hawaiian race. Approximately 18 miles long and six miles wide, Ni'ihau is owned today by the Robinson family, and is home for approximately 250 residents of predominantly Hawaiian ancestry.

*Sunset on Niʻihau.*

*" its rustic, native character "*

*Niʻihau residents greet one another at church on Sunday.*

Niʻihau was purchased in 1864 from King Kamehameha IV by Elizabeth Sinclair, an ancestor of today's owners, when her daughter and son sought a more "adventurous" location for the family's ranching interests. King Kamehameha IV drove a hard bargain, selling the island to the Sinclairs for $10,000 in gold – and, reportedly, Mrs. Sinclair's piano.

Since the occupancy of the island by the Sinclairs, its rustic, native character has been arduously preserved. Today, most of the residents continue to live in simple wooden houses and are employees of the Robinson Ranch. They spend their days herding cattle and sheep, and maintaining the lands. One small elementary school provides education for the younger children. Niʻihau teenagers travel to high schools on Kauaʻi or Oʻahu.

*Ranching is the primary economic activity on Niʻihau.*

*Life's necessities are still handled simply.*

*" bequeathed by members of the Robinson family "*

*Sheep also find a comfortable home on Niʻihau.*

Niʻihau has nevertheless seen its share of activity – including a visit by Captian Cook's shore party in 1778, the landing of a Japanese fighter pilot following the attack on Pearl Harbor in 1941, and the home of a small Coast Guard contingent from 1944 to 1950. Yet even the military personnel were asked to refrain from interrupting the traditional, quiet flow of work and life on Niʻihau. Such a demeanor was required and bequeathed by members of the Robinson family to its heirs.

*Ni'ihau's picturesque coastline.*

*Much of Ni'ihau is still untouched.*

## AN ISLAND OF DRAMATIC CONTRASTS

A thin range of mountains running between Koloa Town and Nāwiliwili Bay provides a dramatic, natural division point for the many faces of Kaua'i. On one side of the range is west Kaua'i where the sun grins its most flirtacious grin, the air is drier, and the land is more arid. This is where surfers and sun bathers play at Po'ipū and nearby points. East Kaua'i boasts Nāwiliwili Harbor and Lihu'e, stretching up into the magical and legendary beauty of Hanalei and Hā'ena.

*Stately, cragged cliffs provide a contrasting backdrop to the velvet cane fields of Kaua'i.*

A dimple in the road, surrounded by a thicket of Hau trees, marks the division point between these contrasting Kaua'i personalities. This location has been the only crossing point for travellers through the mountain ridge since the days of the earliest Hawaiians, and it is easy to notice the change in environment even today.

In earlier days, simply passing through the area frequently struck fear and caution in the heart of wayfarers – particularly on dark nights. Outlaws were known to take refuge in the thick trees and prey on such unsuspecting passers-by.

Robbers however were only a small part of the reason why people feared the "Gap." Spirits of the past were said to have lurked in the shadows – and their intentions were believed to be far more terrifying than those of mere mortal robbers. Even today's travellers notice a mood shift – as they travel back and forth between the two Kaua'is.

This divisive mountain range ends at the southern edge of Nāwiliwili Bay where the opulent Westin Kaua'i Hotel at Kaua'i Lagoons now stands guard over lovely Kalapakī Beach. Nāwiliwili Harbor is Kaua'i's major seaport, welcoming and sending off the freighters and cruise ships to and from the island. Construction on the deep draft harbor began in 1924, was completed by 1930, and has since offered protected berthing for vessels from all over the seafaring world.

*" now stand guard over Kalapakī Beach "*

*A new form of classical elegance now partners with Kauai'i's tropical atmosphere.*

*A swan glides along
a lagoon at the Westin Kaua'i Hotel.*

*A simpler form of transportation than normally
seen escorts visitors to the Westin Kaua'i.*

*Satin fairways beckon
to golfers on the course at Kaua'i Lagoons.*

*" once the sprawling and elegant home "*

Like all of Kaua'i, however, modern commerce exists side by side with ancient history. Resting idly not far from Nāwiliwili's busy and contemporary harbor are the remains of the Alekoko Fish Pond, ancient fishponds reputedly built by the Menehune. This pond is considered to be an important indication of a major aquaculture industry among the ancient Hawaiians. Water from the Hulā'ia River finds its way into the pond through crevices in the walls and specially designed flood gates. The fish grown in the waters, mostly mullet, were food for dignitaries and the Ali'i.

Along the main road to Lihu'e is Kilohana Plantation, once the sprawling and elegant home of plantation owners Gaylord and Ethel Wilcox. Having passed through several uses including operating as a school for delinquents, the historic ranch has been restored to its previous plantation era style, now housing a museum, restaurants and gift shops, and affording a glimpse of the ranch buildings and grounds that were typical of the plantations in early Kaua'i.

*A luxury cruise ship rests in Nāwiliwili Bay.*

*The Kilohana Plantation house provides the perfect shady lawn.*

*The Wailua River criss-crosses through sugar cane fields.*

*" Kaua'i's most rapidly growing area "*

*The traditional crafts are still practiced.*

*Shopping in Kaua'i is a colorful treat.*

Only a few miles away lies Lihu'e, Kaua'i's major commerce center and the point at which most visitors arrive on the island. Lihu'e is Kaua'i's most rapidly growing area because of its central location and its momentum as the central business location. New industrial parks and office buildings are slowly being added to the community. The island's primary shopping center, Kukui Grove, is also located here.

Lihu'e wasn't always the commercial heartbeat of Kaua'i, however. It was a quiet, unnoticed rural area until about 1839 when missionary Dr. Thomas Lafon built a home and took charge of a church. The church had been built at the direction of Kaua'i Governor Kaikioewa, and by 1840 a palace of sorts had been built for the governor's wife. A large school was also built and active by 1840.

*Lihu'e is Kaua'i's commercial center.*

115

*Captain Cook is honored in this monument.*

*Cultivating taro has been carried forth from generation to generation.*

*" white man first stepped foot on Kaua'i "*

*A local woman is dressed for the Kuhio Day celebration.*

A few years later, Henry A. Pierce, sailed into Nāwiliwili Bay and saw the lucrative potential of sugar cane on the hillsides around Lihu'e. Decades later when the potential had become a way of life, activities that supported the endeavour helped add fuel to the commerce in adjacent Lihu'e. Pierce's vision only enhanced that of the former Governor, and would ultimately establish Lihu'e as Kaua'i's county seat and major commerce center.

This side of the island seems a truly distant cousin to the arid hillsides of Waimea and west Kaua'i. Here on the eastern shores, the lands are irrigated by the many rivers and streams from atop Mt. Wai'ale'ale and are therefore more dense with lush foliage, secluded pools and emerald green valleys. A short distance north from Lihu'e lies Wailua – the village, river and valley – and one of the most revered places in all of the Hawaiian Islands.

The white man first stepped foot on Kaua'i on the western shores near Waimea, but here in Wailua the ancient Polynesians first discovered Kaua'i many centuries before, and settled in its mercurially pleasant climate.

The lower Wailua River lands were selected to be the center of activity for these early Hawaiians, for here there was access to water, available fields for harvesting crops, adjacent forests and flat land for homes. The area quickly became the "capital" of the island by choice of the Ali'i and chieftains, and soon became known, along with Waialua on O'ahu, as one of Hawai'i's two most sacred grounds.

*The River cuts a silver course through the valley.*

In the early days, the Wailua River separated and ran in two courses through the valley. Today, the river has reset its own course and covers a specific area deemed by the Hawaiians as sacred, bounded by the valley on both the northern and southern slopes.

*Wailua Nui Hoʻāno* – Great Sacred Wailua – was the name accorded this area by the Aliʻi – and stories of its prominence were reportedly taken back and forth to Tahiti before the 13th century. As a result, the reputation of the great Wailua Valley drew ever more immigrants as the decades passed.

*The ancient hula
is a part of every Hawaiian celebration.*

119

Besides its fame as a congenial place to settle, Wailua also became famous for the sport associated with its flashing surf, for even Polynesians of ancient times enjoyed surfing and were said to have come to Kaua'i in search of good waves.

But not everyone was welcome in Wailua Nui Ho'āno. It was a special place for the Ali'i and only those specifically invited were allowed to partake of the area's pleasures. A canoe landing was designated for vessels of the chieftains, and on the banks where the river merged with the sea, sacred ceremonies were held. Remains of an ancient heiau can still be seen on the southern shore of the River. Called *Hikina a ka lā*, Rising of the Sun, the heiau was said to catch the rays of the morning sun.

*Hikina a ka lā* was a massive structure, of stone, with a large interior divided into three sections. It was known as a Place of Refuge, where individuals who had committed crimes could find safe refuge, perform certain rituals, and be absolved of their wrong-doings. It was also a place of great safety during times of war.

Little remains of this great fortress-like heiau today, but some say that at night, the echo of drums and ancient music still mingles with the thunder of the nearby surf. Another heiau, a short distance away, stands in better condition today than most others on the island. Petroglyphs on the nearby rocks give clues to the intricate past of this area.

Close to the entrance to this most sacred of areas are eight boulders, planted in the entrance to the channel. These boulders are said to be the manifestations of another famous Hawaiian myth which centers around the mischievous demi-god Māui.

*" known as a Place of Refuge "*

*The chants of yesterday recall ancient legends.*

*Petroglyphs offer some of the rare "written" records of the life in ancient Kaua'i.*

*The Place of Refuge provided protection from wars.*

Legend says that this great god chose to draw all the islands together in one mass by fishing for and capturing an under-sea demon, or giant fish, who controlled the lands. To accomplish his task, Māui enlisted the aid of his eight brothers and once they had snagged the demon on their line, they were told not to look back. But they did so anyway, breaking the spell and the line, allowing the islands to be flung far and wide into the Pacific. The sea demon managed to recapture the islands we know today as the islands of Hawai'i, but others such as Tahiti were strewn far away.

As punishment to his brothers for disobeying his order and thereby causing such a near catastrophe, Māui turned the young men into stone and sunk them at the mouth of Wailua River.

A more recent story tells us that Kaua'i's last King, Kaumuali'i, once lived in this area of Wailua, and swam in a nearby pool.

*The sea-demon "one tooth" was said to have held the island chain together in ancient times. Today, scuba divers find "one tooth" like creatures during their explorations underwater.*

*" capturing an under-sea demon, or giant fish "*

Breadfruit was a Hawaiian food staple.

*" toward the top of the sacred volcano "*

The Wailua Valley still celebrates the past.

Kaua'i chiefs would wind their way through the valley upward toward the top of the sacred volcano. Some distance up the pathway from the ocean, under a cliff, are the famous Kaua'i Birthstones, two large pieces of smooth stone, where kings of Kaua'i were delivered from their mothers. A child must be born in this place, Holoholokū, to become king.

Once such a precious child was born, the *kahunas*, or priests, would carry the infant to a ledge overlooking the river, where they would strike a bellstone which signalled the arrival of a new member of the Ali'i. The ringing of these "bells" could be heard throughout the valley.

Seven other heiau are located along the river. *Ka Le o ka Manu*, or The Crest of the Bird, was known as a place of monthly human sacrifice. It was at this heiau that the sharkskin drum was introduced into the ritual – and ultimately evolved into an element used in all hula in the ancient Hawaiian culture.

The legend says that the drum came about when a Kaua'i chieftain, Moikeha, sent his son, Kila, to recover another son born of a lover, Luukia, in Tahiti. Kila not only found the son, but took awesome revenge upon the enemies of his father. Once back in Kaua'i, Kila introduced the drum as a reminder of his own violent activities in Tahiti.

*The path up the valley to the volcano often provides dramatic vistas.*

*The Coco Palms Resort gardens have been a choice place for weddings for many years.*

*" intoxicating strains of the Hawaiian Wedding Song "*

Further up the river is the Malae Heiau which looks across the river and valley and to the Poli'ahu Heiau. Legend says that both heiaus were built by the Menehune, and that Poli'ahu was a most sacred and exclusive place.

Commoners many miles away reported hearing the drums and chants of the gods late into the night – a mysterious phenomenon some say still occurs on occasion even today.

Although these mystical secrets of Kaua'i's past are explored today by adventurers who hike to the sites of the heiaus and historical points, the sunnier aspects of Kaua'i are the most popular charms of this unique island.

Kaua'i's natural beauty, expressed through cascading silver waterfalls, serene rainforests and beautiful panoramas, flirts with travellers through the camera lenses of numerous television series and motion pictures. Millions of visitors yearly boat up the Wailua River to the exotic Fern Grotto where beautiful island voices ring out the intoxicating strains of the Hawaiian Wedding Song, and nuptials are performed daily. The popular boat excursion was begun in 1946 by a taro farmer who saw opportunity in the beauty of the river and its appeal to visitors.

*The Fern Grotto is one of the island's most frequented sights.*

*There are many kinds of sparkling reflections in the waters of Kaua'i.*

127

*The charming lagoon at the Coco Palms Resort.*

*A stroll through the Coco Palms grounds is a walk through time.*

On the beach nearby, several resorts bask lazily at the edge of the surf, among them the famous Coco Palms Resort, a tradition on the island since Grace Guslander took over a bar and grille at the mouth of the river and turned it into one of Hawai'i's first paradise resorts. She converted a 1500 acre plantation, planted originally in 1896, into a stately coconut grove known as "King's Walk," an irrigation canal into a sleepy, tropical lagoon, and created a visitor experience that has since been copied by some of the state's most opulent resorts.

She sent young Hawaiian men running through the plantation, just at twilight, to light tiki torches to the beat of an ancient Polynesian drum. A conch shell was blown as the ceremony got underway, calling guests to dinner – not only from afternoon respites, but from all over the world – to experience what has become one of the most popular of local rituals.

*" to the beat of an ancient Polynesian drum "*

*Kaua'i's most traditional Polynesian hotel.*

*" a reminder of an era in Kaua'i "*

*Antique bottles are among Kapa'a's many interesting collectibles.*

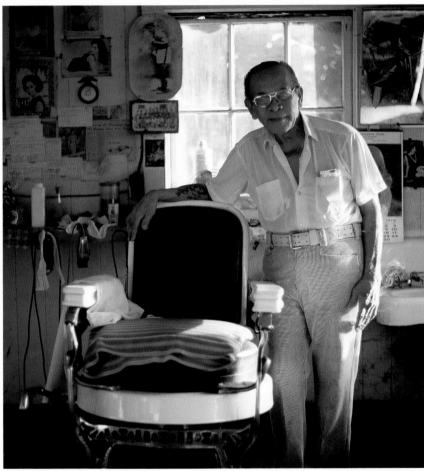

*A barber shop – Kapaʻa style.*

*The General Store.*

On the coast from Wailua northward is a string of sparkling resort hotels and modern shopping conveniences. Kapaʻa is the island's second largest town, and a portrait of the way in which Kauaʻi has married traditional with modern culture. Charming old buildings intermingle with newly built commercial complexes and create a center that has become home to an international community. Kapaʻa, like its neighbor to the north, Keālia, was once a plantation center. Today, little is left of the village but a reminder of an era in Kauaʻi that has come and gone.

*"Sleeping Giant" mountain is a Menehune fable.*

*Children tumble along the Alaka'i SwampTrail to find muddy fun.*

Even with the emphasis and activity focused away from sugar and agriculture, a rural lifestyle surrounds even the busiest commerce centers. Just inland from Keālia, laughing *keikis* hike through a field to reach Waipahee Slide – an eroded lava tube which tumbles down a steep slope into a cool, crystal pool nearly 20 feet deep. Water – and children sliding along its surface – have made the slide a quick, exhilarating afternoon pastime – one which has been enjoyed by local Kauaians for centuries. Today it is necessary to obtain a permit from the Lihu'e Plantation to hike into the slide

Keeping watch over this shore's resort centers is the imposing mountain called "Sleeping Giant." According to legend, a giant fell into such a deep sleep that when the Menehune attempted to waken him by throwing rocks at him, he swallowed the stones and never awakened, turning into a stone mountain.

Unspoiled beaches dot the coastline here – from Anahola to the secluded beauty of Moloa'a, where white clouds float over an untouched beach and small tide pools are warmed by the morning sun. Sometimes three or four white horses graze quietly in the fields skirting this pristine beach.

Whether it's the gentle embrace of a sparkling sandy beach, busy Lihu'e or the bustle of the energetic resorts along this coast, all are congenial neighbors with ancient and sacred grounds along the Wailua River. All reflect the unique and enchanting spirit of Kaua'i that has warmly welcomed beauty and peace seekers since the earliest times.

*The people of Kaua'i present a colorful and happy lifestyle.*

133

## MAGICAL CHANTS AND SENSUOUS DANCES – KAUA'I'S MYSTICAL NORTH SHORE

If beauty is the measure of the perfect Hawaiian haven, then surely Kaua'i's north shore is the jewel in the crown. From its gossamer silhouette at twilight, to the velvet mosses that cover its pathways, here is a portrait of beauty that could only have been painted by a Master.

*Kaua'i's North Shore.*

*" once guided ships from the Orient around the coast "*

Here on the North Shore especially, history partners with contemporary life to create Kaua'i's most appealing character. The Kīlauea Plantation, located at the gateway to the Hanalei shore, was built in the 1870s, and although it has long been closed, its heart still beats affectionately within the bosom of the historic community of Kīlauea.

The town itself is a charming reminder of yesterday's lifestyle on Kaua'i, with stone buildings located throughout the small town, including a most interesting plantation manager's residence that was built in 1928. Standing watch over the Pacific Ocean is the Kīlauea Lighthouse, high on a plateau above the water. Constructed with a unique clam-shell lens, the light once guided ships from the Orient around the coast of Kaua'i. Although no longer active, the historic tower is now an imposing sentry over a wildlife refuge that many unusual seabirds call home. Among them are the Blue Faced Boobies who provide entertainment for visitors with their happy-go-lucky frolicking and graceful dives.

Nearby is the unique Guava Kai Plantation, 480 acres of guava trees, a processing plant and visitor center.

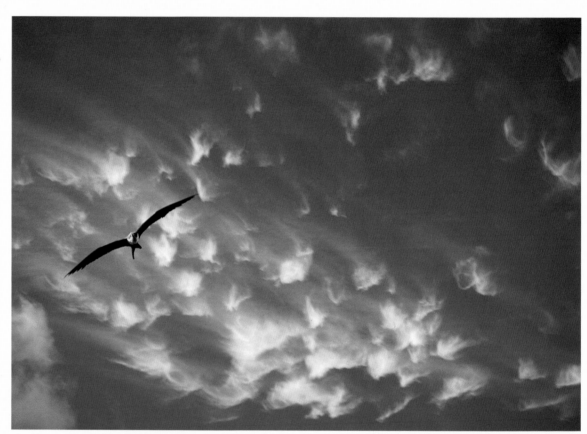

*An 'Iwa soars above the North Shore coastline.*

*The Kīlauea Lighthouse keeps vigil over the Pacific.*

*Princeville Hotel captured the vision of early Kaua'i entrepreneurs.*

## " once a historic plantation "

Not far from Kīlauea, what was once a historic plantation spread across a long, high plateau has today become a beacon of modern carefree resort living. Princeville at Hanalei is a planned resort community opened in 1968 on property that was originally part of the Princeville Ranch, Kauaʻi's largest ranch.

*The excitement of polo has found its way to Kauaʻi .*

*The feathery Hāipu blows in the breeze.*

*" he entertained royalty and renowned visitors "*

*One of the many textures of Kauaʻi's agriculture.*

The legacy of the Princeville Ranch is a bitter-sweet tale. It involved the dream of Scotsman Robert Crichton Wyllie who envisioned miles and miles of sugar cane blowing in the trade winds, and large revenues as a result. In keeping with this dream, he built in 1853 one of the most elaborate sugar mill operations in the state. Machinery was imported from Germany, and a fleet of barges took the cane down the Hanalei River for processing. The mill would personify Wyllie's own grand style and his dream – but only for a few years.

The rains and resultant wet earth kept the area from being an ideal cane growing location. Yields were never as plentiful as Wyllie had envisioned, or as they were in dryer locations. Nonetheless, Wyllie's reputation as one of the island's most genteel growers remained with him as he entertained royalty and renowned visitors, continuing to awe his fellow trades-people with his showpiece mill.

*The McBryde Sugar Mill continues to operate today.*

*Life at Princeville was intended to be genteel and pleasant .*

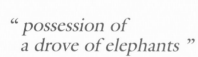

*" possession of
a drove of elephants "*

Only upon his death, in 1865, and the appointment of a distant relative as his heir, did the financial reality of the operation become known. Mortgages against the property abounded, and one account claimed, "...the inheritance was like coming into possession of a drove of elephants."

The young cousin, so distraught over his newly gained financial plight, cut his own throat and died. The plantation and mill for which Wyllie had paid approximately $200,000, was auctioned for barely $80,000. With no legacy left to perpetuate it, the name Wyllie quietly disappeared.

*Visitors and residents at Princeville*
*today have recaptured the dream of tropical elegance.*

*" during the days
of the ancient Hawaiians "*

Princeville Ranch, and the valley which surrounds it, however, is an important part of Kaua'i's history. It was the first ranch developed on the island, and attempts to make it profitable as a plantation over the years are textbook studies in frustration. For a time even sheep were raised on the land. As early as 1865, ethnic battles took place when laborers from two different Chinese provinces entangled.

The sprawling resort that now occupies this placid area of the Hanalei Valley is a fitting legacy, however, to Wyllie's earliest dreams of an elegant, genteel lifestyle.

By 1930, the Hanalei Valley had become a busy rice producing area. In 1924 the Haraguchi Rice Mill was opened and operated until about 1960. Rice was shipped through Hanalei Bay at the time. Since the demise of that agricultural industry, Hanalei has returned to the kind of quiet life it enjoyed during the days of the ancient Hawaiians.

A rustic steel bridge built in 1912 is still the only entry into Hanalei – a fitting gateway to one of the island's most peaceful and historic locations. Hanalei today remains a small village blanketed by a lush, emerald jungle.

*The placid Hanalei Valley.*          145

*" founded a mission and adjacent church "*

Only a short distance up the road is charming Wai'oli where Protestant missionaries founded a mission and adjacent church on the banks of the Wai'oli River. At this point, the journey into Kaua'i's ancient-most past begins – and lives today. The road narrows, crosses numerous timeworn bridges, and skirts enchanting, secluded beaches.

Lovely Wainiha fronts a valley where dense foliage mingles with a never-ending system of waterfalls that provide a good deal of the island's power. A community of native Hawaiians also live here.

*The bloodlines of Hawai'i
are evident in the faces of Hanalei area residents.*

*The Wai'oli Mission Church in Hanalei.*

*A catamaran slices across the sunny horizon at Wainiha Bay.*

*" she dreamt of Kauaʻi "*

*Ancient Polynesians revered their own gods.*

Soon the road comes to an appropriate conclusion at Hā'ena – a shoreline revered as one of the most magical, immortalized through the Bali Hai sequences in the movie "South Pacific," and through legends that take us back centuries before the invention of film. This is the location of three legendary lava tubes, known as Manini-holo Dry Cave, Waikapala'e Wet Cave and Wai-kanaloa Wet Cave, said to have been dug by Pele.

The great goddess of fire sought her first Hawaiian home adjacent to lovely Hā'ena. She dug a cave with the intention of settling, but when she hit water there, and again in another nearby cave, she gave up the idea and travelled the islands until she discovered the volcanic heat on the Big Island of Hawai'i. Later, deep in slumber, and listening to the chanting of her sister Hi'iaka, she dreamt of Kaua'i, and heard drum beats signaling an elaborate festival.

*Hawaiian women at a hula performance in Hā'ena.*

*" the throbbing of the drums."*

Pele's spirit travelled to the celebration where her fiery heart was smitten by the powerful presence of Lohi'au, the chieftain in charge of the event. A great passion developed between them as they danced to the throbbing of drums.

Pele was obliged to return to her home and awaken, but vowed to send for Lohi'au. He grew more and more despondent over her departure and believing that he would never see her again, hung himself.

When Pele awoke, back at home on Hawai'i, she bid Hi'iaka to travel to Kaua'i and bring Lohi'au to her. Hi'iaka arrived at Hā'ena only to find that Lohi'au was dead. She captured his spirit and forced it back into his body, restoring him to life. As the two journeyed to Hawai'i and Pele, they fell in love.

When Pele discovered the lovers, a long skirmish developed between the two sisters. It was a conflict that saw Pele covering Hi'iaka and Lohi'au with lava, miraculous resurection to life and many legends written of the conflict.

Suffice it to say, so distressed was Pele over the lovers that her fury and anger is said to keep the volcano fires burning even today.

*Early Polynesians travelled via canoes.*

*A Kauaʻi resident accompanies a traditional hula performance.*

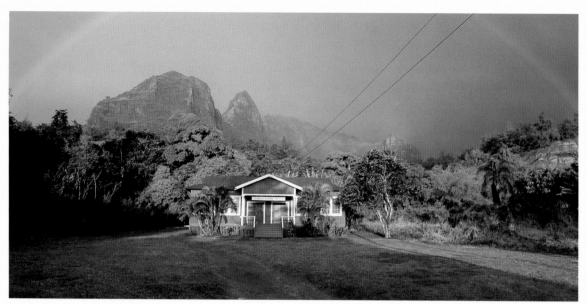

*The Anahola Baptist Church.*

Another legend tells of Kilioe, mistress of Laka's hula hālau at Hāʻena, who was awakened in the darkness of night by the call of a small lizard signaling activity near the hālau. Kilioe ventured out to explore the sounds and caught a glimpse of two lovers who were her students, forbidden to be seen on this special night just before their graduation. As she followed the lovers across a stream, seeking to chastise them for breaking the rules, they noticed her and, frightened of her power, fled.

*" followed the lovers across a stream "*

*Kumu Hulas*
*continue to preserve cultural traditions.*

*Legends aside, the annual Stampede in Hanalei retains the flavor of historic Kaua'i.*

*" a cave forged by the swirling surf "*

One of the young lovers, Nanau, realized that escape was fruitless and told his beloved Kapaka to hide in a cave forged by the swirling surf. His intention was to distract Kilioe from punishing Kapaka, but as he climbed a nearby rise, Kapaka emerged from her hiding place and called to her pursuer. She was swiftly struck down by Kilioe's club. Kilioe then pursued Nanau up the hill and struck him down as well.

*The caves on Kaua'i's shoreline are an integral part of all her legends.*

*A timeless sun watches over Kaua'i's paddlers.*

*Flowers have adorned the hair and necks of Kaua'i's children from the earliest times.*

*Dancers prepare for a luau performance.*

*" ancient chants and dances of their ancestors "*

The next day, fishermen reported the appearance of an unusual and new plant on the spot where Kapaka had fallen. It bore a tiny bud shaped like a half-teardrop. Bird hunters discovered another new plant on the slopes above the beach. It, too bore a half-flower. Kilioe placed two buds together and saw that the gods had marked the death of these two lovers with two separate plants that grew on the places of their deaths.

Hā'ena visitors and residents are still enchanted by the tiny, unique plants that grow separately near the beach, and then again on the slopes.

Dance hālaus today occasionally use these historic grounds to perform the ancient chants and dances of their ancestors.

*Hawaiian children learn traditional crafts at an early age.*

157

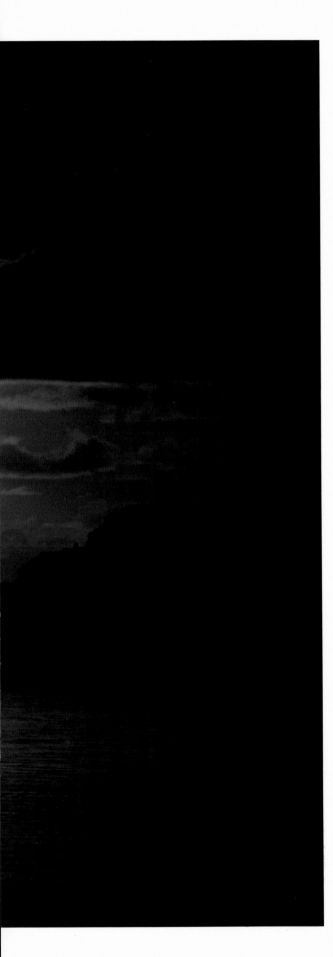

*" dramatic end of the road "*

This revered site is a fitting and dramatic end of the road on the shoreline of Kauaʻi. Here, the jagged cliffs of the Nā Pali Coast take over the island, providing a breathtaking exclamation to the fascinating history and legends so vividly reflected in Hanalei and Hāʻena.

*Kauaʻi's North Shore has proven to be a magical place for those who visit or live there.*

## NĀ PALI COAST –
## NATURE MAKES HER MARK

There is a stormy romance, indeed a sensuous mating among the many elements of nature, that takes place day and night along the breath-taking coastline of Kaua'i known as Nā Pali. Dark, jagged cliffs rise nearly 3,000 feet above the boiling waves that crash against their base, and constant winds and rain pelt away at the rocky surfaces. High atop Nā Pali is Mount Wai'ale'ale, where swamps and bogs catch more annual rainfall than any other place on earth.

But on sunny days along the shoreline, the sun's rays caress the white sandy inlets and the fern-covered slopes of the valleys embraced by the cliffs. Seabirds, wild pigs and other rare wildlife busy themselves in the noonday warmth, and the relatively few humans who have the tenacity to explore this remote wilderness attest to the fact that it is perhaps the most naturally luxurious tropical paradise anywhere.

*Hā'ena Beach's mysterious tunnels where Pele first sought a home – gateway to the drama of Nā Pali.*

*Breathtaking beauty is the trademark of the Nā Pali coastline.*

*" began as gentle slopes "*

*Jagged outcrops of rock pierce the horizon.*

The sentry-like cliffs that keep the Nā Pali Coast remote and venerable today were carved by centuries of sea and weather pounding away at what began as gentle slopes from the top of the mountain. Over time, deeply creviced vertical palisades were etched, caves hollowed, and valleys formed.

*The Kalalau Valley – background of many Kauaʻi legends and stories.*

*" along the sparkling beaches "*

Access to this magnificent area is by boat or
hiking trails only – and has been so since the
arrival of the first Polynesians. A trail nearly
eleven miles long leads hikers into the hidden
valleys and along the sparkling beaches. It is part
of a system of trails used by the ancient Hawaiians, leading them into small terraced taro farms
that existed centuries before Captain Cook or
the missionaries ventured to Kaua'i.

*The beauty of Kaua'i's coast is striking from any angle.*

*" the less accessible valleys "*

*Surf fishing along the Nā Pali coast is basically as it was one hundred years ago.*

The trail begins at Ke'e Beach, part of Hā'ena
State Park, climbs a steep slope, and descends
into Hanakāpī'ai Valley. Here, casual hikers bring
picnic lunches to spend several hours in the sun,
returning to their cars at Ke'e after a short but
exhilarating walk. Reaching the less accessible
valleys takes more stamina and confidence.

Further along the trail, Ho'olau and Waiahuakau
Valleys precede the lovely Hanakoa Valley. There,
a waterfall tumbles into a cool deep stream. Ardu-
ous climbing along a pathway that switches back
and forth along the steep ridges, and endures
constant assaults of rain and rockslides, leads to
the Nā Pali's most secluded and legend-bound
valley, Kalalau.

*Cool mountain waters tumble over the rocks and
down the slopes of the Kalalau Valley.*

167

*An entire community of farmers, hunters and fishermen has disappeared from the Kalalau Valley .*

*" had died or moved on "*

Known as the "Valley of the Lost Tribe," this was a place of refuge and safety for centuries. It is said that a large community of farmers, hunters and fishermen lived in the Kalalau Valley for nearly a thousand years. With the protection of the cliffs and coastline, this community was left to thrive on its own without threat from outside influence or invasion. Yet by the early 1900s, the inhabitants had died or moved on to more active communities, and only a few taro patches remained.

*Hula dancers re-enact the legends of the Nā Pali coast.*

*The spectacular Kalalau Valley.*

The Makaweli Ranch, owned by the Robinson family which also owns the island of Ni'ihau, has grazed its cattle on some of the lands in this area for the past few decades, but by and large, only hearty hikers have kept the vigil in this spectacular valley. A few nature-dedicated hermits have also found the solace and seclusion of Kalalau to be singularly important in their lives.

One such refugee was Ko'olau, a young paniolo, who with his wife and son ran away from their Waimea home in 1883, when they learned that both father and son had contracted Hansen's disease, then called leprosy. They discovered a colony of lepers in the Kalalau Valley who, like themselves, were unwilling to move to the leper colony on the island of Moloka'i.

In the early 1890s, a Kaua'i Deputy Sheriff ventured into the valley to confront the lepers and convince them to leave. A skirmish developed between the deputy and Ko'olau and when it ended, the lawman had been shot to death. Kaua'i government officials arrived at the mouth of the valley by steamer, with a "posse" of policemen and National Guardsmen, and captured the colony – except for Ko'olau who escaped.

The outlaw paniolo remained uncaptured in the valley along with his family until 1896 when he and his son died and were buried there. The wife returned to her Waimea home, after which the family's story was fictionalized by author Jack London in his short story, "Ko'olau The Leper".

*A luxury cruise ship is only a speck on the horizon against the mighty Nā Pali cliffs.*

*" fictionalized by author Jack London "*

Kalalau Valley views have inspired many naturalists.

The Kaumakani Church has seen generations of Kauaians

*Helicopter tours*
*provide a bird's-eye view of Nā Pali's splendor.*

*" of all the requirements for survival, beauty is the most important "*

Another Kalalau refugee was Dr. Bernard Wheatley, a black physician from the Virgin Islands who first discovered the Valley in the mid 1950s and was so smitten with its beauty and serenity, he made a cave his home. No distant esthete was this learned man. He knew people would question his actions and met the criticism head on. Over the years he would invite hikers to stay in his cave and share his meals. But he also established a set of rules for proper behavior in this most revered valley – rules designed to protect the delicate balance of nature Wheatley so loved.

"I have found," said Wheatley, "that of all the requirements for survival, beauty is the most important." Taro, mangoes and other indigenous fruits and vegetation along with wildlife of the area were Wheatley's food. Waterfalls provided his showers.

So respected was this nature-lover that whenever he ventured out of the valley, he was always picked up and delivered to his intended destination by local residents, or given a place to stay until he returned to his home.

Wheatley lived in the Kalalau Valley for many years before he bade a permanent farewell, explaining that the traffic created by hikers and sightseers had fouled the environment for him.

*The waters off the coast attract many visitors.*            *Nā Pali's beaches are still secluded and untouched .*

*" many fluorescent fish and underwater creatures "*

Underwater explorers are likely to meet an octopus.

A colorful palette of fish escort the divers off Nā Pali's coast.

A manta ray regards the camera with curiosity.

Such a concern has been expressed by others with a less intimate knowledge of the dramatic Nā Pali Coast. Government officials along with conservationists keep a watchful eye today on the effect of the boating and helicopter tours that bring visitors to sample the delicacies of the area.

And many are the delicacies to be enjoyed, from the frolicsome migration of the giant humpback whales to the rainbow hues of the many fluorescent fish and underwater creatures just off the coast, to the velvet green blankets of foliage and silvery threads of waterfalls embroidered within it.

*Even the humpback whale plays along the dramatic Nā Pali shoreline.*

*" snorkel, sunbask and explore "*

*Rubber dinghies are a popular way to see the coastline.*

*A sea urchin in a tidepool greets a small explorer.*

Recreational boats churn their way to the quiet beaches along the face of the massive cliffs where island visitors snorkel, sunbask and explore in relative privacy. Helicopter tours provide a sweeping view of these imposing palisades and the fascinating natural treasurers hiding in their crevices.

*Caves and coves provide fascinating exploring for Nā Pali visitors who are adventurous.*

A fifteen-mile expanse of coastline from
Hā'ena State Park to Polihale State Park
on the western shore of Kaua'i, and from
Hā'ena to Kōke'e State Park inland, the
Nā Pali Coast will stand forever as the gate
to Hawai'i's Eden.

# INFINITE REFLECTIONS

"…of all the requirements for survival, beauty is the most important," said well known Kauai naturalist and hermit Dr. Bernard Wheatley.

Such is the allure of the Garden Island of Kaua'i – a radiance that brought the earliest visitors from Polynesia to the Hawaiian Islands. It is the beauty etched in the mossy valleys and along the secluded beaches of Kaua'i, that sparkles from the waterfalls and smiles from the sunlit surf.

The people of Kaua'i know their island home is unique, and they carry a deep cultural pride. Theirs was one of the earliest of the Hawaiian Islands to be populated and one of the last to integrate itself into the political structure emanating from Honolulu.

Today's visitors to Kaua'i are struck not only by its beauty, but by the warmth of its people, eloquently communicating the spirit of a more distant and peaceful culture, creating the intoxicating reflection of Kaua'i.

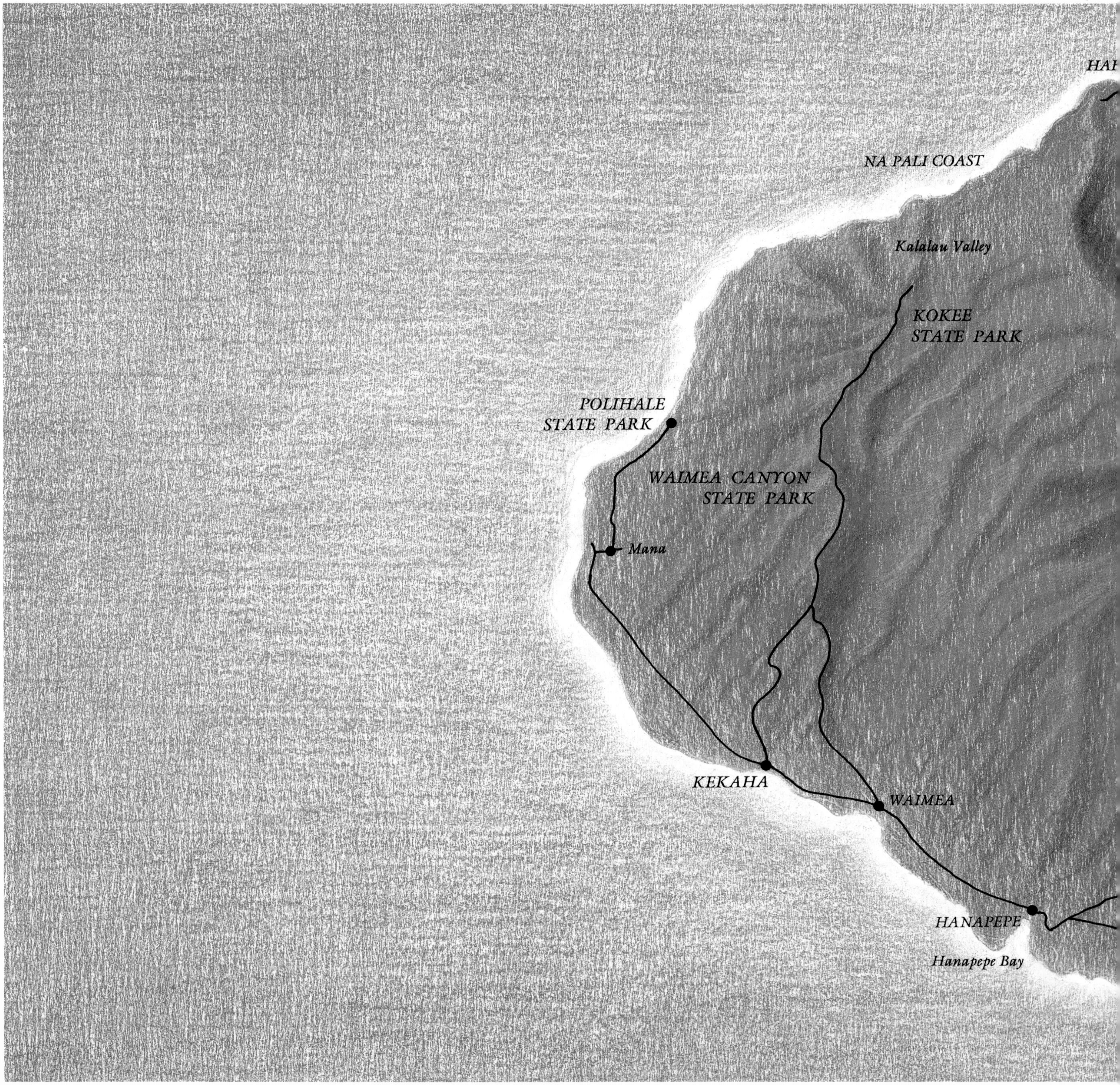

HAI
NA PALI COAST
Kalalau Valley
KOKEE
STATE PARK
POLIHALE
STATE PARK
WAIMEA CANYON
STATE PARK
Mana
KEKAHA
WAIMEA
HANAPEPE
Hanapepe Bay

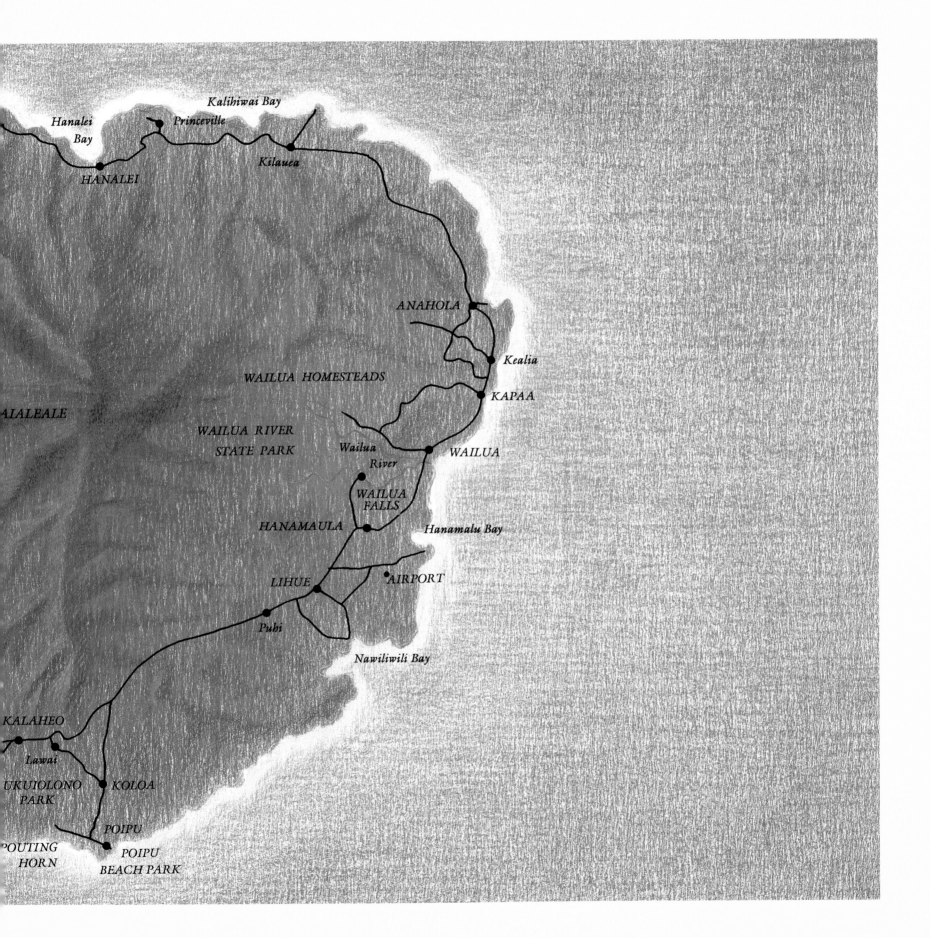

## ACKNOWLEDGING THOSE PHOTOGRAPHIC ARTISTS WHO HAVE CAPTURED THE SPIRIT AND BEAUTY OF KAUA'I

PHOTOGRAPHERS - DRAMATIC CONTRASTS

109   Keith Karasic

111   Sun Star  L/C *
      Gary Hofheimer  R/U/C
      Sun Star  R/L/C
      J. L. Carini  R*

113   David Boynton  L
      Steven Gnazzo/ Kilohana  R

115   Greg Vaughn  L
      Brett Uprichard  L/U/C
      Brett Uprichard  R/U/C *
      Greg Vaughn  R/C*

117   David Boynton  L
      Mike Teruya  L/C
      Gerald Ida  R

119   Dane Warner  L/C
      Brett Uprichard  U/R *

121   David Boynton  L
      Mike Teruya  C
      David Boynton  R

123   Ed Robinson  C
      David Boynton  R *

125   David Boynton  L
      David Boynton  R

127   Greg Vaughn  L
      Coco Palms Resort  U/L **
      Peter French  R

129   Coco Palms Resort  L**
      Peter French  L/C *
      Coco Palms Resort  R **

131   Nobu Nakayama  L
      Turner & deVries  C
      Brett Uprichard  R *

133   Peter French  L
      David Boynton  U/R
      David Boynton  L/R

PHOTOGRAPHERS - MAGICAL CHANTS
AND SENSUOUS DANCES

135   David Boynton  C

137   David Boynton  L
      Peter French  R

139   Princeville Hotel  L
      David Boynton  R

141   David Boynton  L/L
      David Boynton  U/L
      David Boynton  R

143   Princeville Hotel  L
      Princeville Hotel  R

145   Peter French  C

147   David Boynton  L
      Greg Vaughn  L/C
      Nobu Nakayama  R

149   David Boynton  L
      David Boynton  R

151   Mike Horikawa  L *
      David Boynton  R

153   Mike Teruya  U/L
      David Boynton  L/L
      David Boynton  R

155   Peter French  L *
      David Boynton  R

157   Ann Cecil  L *
      J. Davis  R/C *
      David Boynton  R

159   Nobu Nakayama  C

PHOTOGRAPHERS - THE NĀ PALI COAST

161   Peter French  L
      Greg Vaughn  R

163   Linda Rulli  L
      Greg Vaughn  R

165   Greg Vaughn  C

167   Mike Teruya  L
      Peter French  R

169   Don King  L
      Greg Vaughn  C
      Mike Teruya  R

171   Greg Vaughn  L
      Mike Teruya  U/R
      Greg Vaughn  L/R

173   Island Helicopters Kaua'i  U/L
      Don King  U/L/C
      Peter French  C

175   Ed Robinson  L
      Ed Robinson  C/R
      Ed Robinson  U/R
      Ed Robinson  L/R

177   Gary Hofheimer  U/L
      Ed Robinson  L/L
      Don King  R

179   Mike Teruya  C

PHOTOGRAPHERS - INFINITE REFLECTIONS

181   Sheraton Hotels  L

PHOTOGRAPHERS - SATELLITE PAGE

      U. S. Geological Survey – EROS

SPECIAL THANKS TO THE FOLLOWING FOR THEIR
GENEROUS PHOTOGRAPHIC CONTRIBUTIONS:

      Bishop Museum Photographic Archives
      Waioli Mission House / Grove Farm Homestead
      Sheraton Hotels
      Coco Palms Resort
      Kilohana Plantation
      Island Helicopters Kaua'i

* Courtesy of Stock Photos Hawaii
** Courtesy Patti Cook and Associates

# BIBLIOGRAPHY

ESSENTIAL GUIDE TO KAUA'I
Ruth Gurnani-Smith
Island Heritage Publishing,
a division of The Madden Corporation
Honolulu, Hawaii
First Edition
Copyright 1988

THE HAWAIIANS
Gavan Daws and Ed Sheehan
Island Heritage Publishing,
a division of The Madden Corporation
Honolulu, Hawaii
Fourth Edition 1970

LETTERS FROM THE SANDWICH ISLANDS
Edited by Joan Abramson
Island Heritage, Ltd.
Norfok Island, Australia - 1975

KAUA'I
The Separate Kingdom
Edward Joesting
University of Hawaii Press
Paperback edition 1987

KAUA'I
Bob Krause, Bill Gleaner
Island Heritage Publishing,
a division of The Madden Corporation
Honolulu, Hawaii
Fifth Edition, 1986
Copyright 1987

KAUA'I
A Many Splendored Island
Douglas Peebles, Ronn Ronck
Mutual Publishing of Honolulu
Copyright 1985

KAUA'I
Hawai'i's Garden island
Robert Wenkam
Tradewinds Publishing, Deerfield, Ill.
Copyright 1979

NI'IHAU
The Last Hawaiian Island
Ruth M. Tabrah
Press Pacifica, Kailua, Hawaii
Copyright 1987

Remarks on "The Tour Around
Hawai'i" by the Missionairies
Ellis, Thurston, Bishop & Goodrich in 1823
Printed for the Authors - Salem 1848

ROAMING IN HAWAI'I
Harry A. Franck
Frederick A. Stokes Co.
New York, N.Y. - 1937

THE WILCOX QUILTS IN HAWAI'I
Robert J. Schleck
Grove Farm Homestead and Waioli Mission House
Hawaii, 1986

# INDEX